Dear

I really hope you enjoy the book,

all the best,

love to you

Delia xx.

Making Marks

Musings of A Curious Mind

Delia Pring

1st Edition

ALL RIGHTS RESERVED

Copyright 2021 LilyMoore Publishing

ISBN: 9781638486374

All rights reserved. No part of this book may be reproduced in any form or by any electronic or mechanical means, including information storage and retrieval systems, without permission in writing from the publisher, except by A reviewer who may quote brief passages in a review.

With the exception of quotes used in reviews, this book may not be reproduced or used in whole or part by any means existing without written permission from the publisher, LilyMoore Publishing, Contact: lilymoorepublishing@gmail.com Bristol, United Kingdom.

Warning: The unauthorised reproduction of this copyrighted work is illegal. No part of this book may be scanned, uploaded, or distributed via the internet or any other means, electronic or print, without the publisher's permission. Criminal copyright infringement without monetary gain, is investigated by the FBI and is punishable by up to five years in federal prison and fine of up to

$250,000.

lilymoorepublishing.com

Contents

- Abstract
- Robins' Nests and Sea Shells
- Sunrise to the Sound of Bubbles
- Dead Zoo
- Evelyn
- Whole House
- Becoming Fantastic
- Tea With Grandma Jean
- Rich in Shit
- Left Hand Path
- Why Weight

For Blossom

Your life has marked you in unique ways, and these marks – whether you know it or not - will determine how you live your life, what quests you pursue, and what you are equipped to say with passion and authority.

- Michael Rabinger.

Abstract

Making Marks is an anthology that explores multiple subjects, narrative techniques, and the multifaceted nature of my experiences. It utilises experimentation, free from the bonds of chronology and traditional structure. Within these pieces, I explore some pivotal times in my life. Those marks have shaped and created me. Moulded, manipulated, and scarred.

Within the writing ideas of identity, self-reflection curiosity and life are explored through some experimental writing and traditional methods. Focusing on objects and emotional responses the portfolio considers what creates the individual. What moulds our perceptions and our personalities and how we are influenced by the wider landscape.

I discovered objects hold huge significance. Here I celebrate them and consider them beyond their physical form. Tactile, with multiple layers *Making Marks* reflects upon curiosity and a search for experiences and explanations. Offering the reader alternative viewpoints and providing the opportunity for questions.

Each piece is individual. They meander through time and place. Differ in tone, content, length and visual presentation. Connections are made through subtle weavings of motif, theme and repetition. Each of these pieces is a singular entity. Created to arouse questions and seek meaning for the author and audience. Together the portfolio illustrates a wider sphere of curiosity, enquiry and desire for understanding.

As individual pieces, each encapsulates an aspect of my life. Together they create a multi-layered picture bringing together attributes of memoir, social commentary, verbatim and nature writing.

I have researched extensively to inform and create deeper connotations for some of the pieces. Yet the research is woven into the larger picture the work evokes. The research underpins my knowledge and places the anthology within the wider landscape. I have used extracts from newspaper reports, including the Siberian Times, and The Express and Echo. The RAMM in Exeter has been crucial to locating these primary sources.

The breadth of subjects within *Making Marks* illustrates snippets of a life. One that continues to evolve and experience. One that will continue to question, learn, and collect.

Robins Nests and Seashells

Animals do not judge; they listen with little response. Hours spent with my horse; her hoof beats a rhythm accompanying my rambling soliloquies.

As bullying became worse, I retreated to books and art, stayed quietly at the sides of the playground collecting bugs. My favourites being those tiny round yellow-green insects that make a gob of cuckoos' spit to hide within. They fascinated me more than caterpillars and tadpoles. I couldn't comprehend how such a tiny creature could make such a comparatively vast ball of moisture within which to reside.

Where did it all come from? I spent a lot of time in my own company and was very comfortable within my imagination. Those who were cruel were turned into fairy tale villains or monsters who had cursed me to live this way because secretly I was someone else.

I had no interest in playing with dolls or a house. A beautiful pram I was given was remodelled into a mobile worm farm specifically to feed the garden birds. My room was full of jars and tanks containing various bugs and snails, tadpoles scooped from the craters of upturned trees. Hours spent trudging through damp woodlands to specific areas just to collect frogspawn. This miraculous translucent jelly with its central black speck promising to become a frog. Jars glistening with the hope of frogs on my window sill, quietly cooking in the sunlight. Tadpoles gasped at thick fuggy air, shadows forging their way through a soup of algae and excrement until I was finally bribed to release them into a large concrete water butt.

I would build little ramps and ladders that descended into the water allowing them to escape once they had transformed into their adult form. My mind filled with the complexities of nature, awash with birdsong and dappled sunlight. I wanted to explore. To learn, feel and understand how it worked. Incarcerated in my jars and tanks I kept a myriad of wonders. Glittering beetles scurried through moistened earth and moss, caterpillars stoically chewed through brussel sprout tops and ragwort, their droppings pungent and putrid at the bottom of the stems. Snails of all sizes and colours were numbered and catalogued in notebooks where I would record their movements, eating habits and inevitable deaths. Most of my animals died and undoubtedly suffered terribly in their tiny prisons.

Growing up surrounded by animals means that their absence is both alien and a novelty. Our home was always filled with various creatures and was lovingly nicknamed 'Menagerie Manor', all we needed was a jersey cow and a couple of lambs and we could have opened our very own petting zoo. Large cages occupied areas of the garden boasting ferrets, Guineas pigs, long silky eared lop rabbits and tiny fluffy dwarf lion heads hopped around their runs. Aviaries boasted a plethora of musical feathered jewels. Colours flittered behind the wire as these imprisoned beauties lived their rather entangled lives in my care.

I have always enjoyed watching birds, it is an activity I still engage in as I go about mundane routines. My Grandma Bumble introduced me to the birds with the magical gift of a pair of old binoculars. I felt like Phileas Fogg peering into a world of wonders magnified and filling my infantile imagination. Cold brass beautifully moulded and rather unforgiving eyepieces expanded and retreated into stumpy, bell-shaped tunnels topped with shiny yet scratched domed lenses. They reminded me of shrunken elephant's feet, like the ones in stately homes. Hollowed out and rimmed with metal or topped with a cushion.

    Hours would be spent in the garden digging worms to try and entice the birds out from their hiding places. I would crunch my binoculars into my eye sockets and study the colours and structures of their feathers. Flashes of blues, oranges, yellows, and brown amongst the leaves. The delicate differences amongst species. I loved blue tits, coal tits and the great tits that would dangle from the bird feeders. Flashes of blue, yellow, and black skittering amongst the hedges. Delicate beaks extracting morsels as they perform skilful acrobatics. Song thrushes would fill the air with music and others would join the medley. The wildness of these tiny beings was counterbalanced by their need to visit our bird tables. A fair exchange, I got to enjoy their company for a fee of peanuts, seed and a bunch of sacrificial earthworms. Some choose to spend their time with you. There was a particularly forthright Robin who would dive into the earth you were turning to extract startled invertebrates. 'Cheeky Chappie' he was affectionately christened. We must have gone through five or six incarnations of this little character. He graced Bumbles garden for at least fifteen years, remarkable for a bird who only has an average lifespan of two years. More remarkable was 'Cheeky Chappies' attachment to my grandma as he followed her across town when she moved house. Her delight as he perched expectantly as ever on the long-handled fork as she rummaged around amongst the myriad of weeds her new garden had greeted her with.

    twiddle-oo, twiddle-eedee, twiddle-oo twiddle.

    Their song alters throughout the year from a melancholy warble in winter to a chirpier trill as breeding season approaches. There is also a belief that a robin close by indicates a deceased love one is near, similar to the appearance of white feathers in unexpected places. My grandma took great comfort in this. She was never alone in her garden. Now I have an assortment of white feathers, tokens of her presence.

tititic, tititic, tititic

One of the advantages of horse ownership is it tends to be a rural activity, as such the proximity to wildlife allows for regular chances to watch and be watched. Every yard has its own robin. A splash of red whipping amongst the hay and horses. Old habits die hard as I clamber the dung heap, sink the fork into the moist heavy substance and turn it over revealing squiggling pink bodies writhing in the warmth of the rotting muck. The little bird makes its choices and then flies away, totally free and unaware of my gaze.

I collect experiences with wildlife as it breathes and dies. Seasons called in by the first sighting of a swift ducking amongst the buttercups, the smell of cut hay, engorged blackberries glowing in the hedges. The hunched form of a buzzard, his back to the wind, curved talons anchored to the gatepost. Ruffled feathers watchful, waiting for the Sunday roast chicken carcass, a gift in the scarcity of winter. These moments ticked off, an inner photograph album thumbed through regularly.

I had a jar of iridescent beetle shells. They rattled paper-thin, delicate echoes of their former duty. In the sunlight, they glisten purple and blue reminiscent of oil shimmering in a puddle. I would actively search for these beetles who reside in horse manure. Dwelling within tunnels they forge through the excrement and into the ground. I was more likely to find them in manure that was a couple of days old and armed with a trowel and ice cream tub and I would hunt them down. It's remarkable the amount of life you can find in a pile of faeces. Not only the oil shelled beetles but earthworms, grubs and tiny black beetles that break down the dung and scurry away from sunlight. They always gather at the bottom of the wheelbarrow when I cleaned the paddocks. Unceremoniously shaken from the metal onto the muckheap where they would clamour over each other to rebury themselves before they were picked by beady-eyed birds. So many jars of beetle shells. Ladybirds of different shades and spot counts, pincer tailed earwigs, segmented woodlice, acid green shield bugs, fluffy soft bumble bees with minute shimmering wings which should never have been able to propel them busily from flower to flower. Then there were shells. Not just eggshells, but snail shells, seashells. Pieces of shells. Crab claws with their sinewy joints dried to a papery film. My favourites were muscle shells, whose smooth insides felt like silk and shimmered like pearls. I considered myself a collector. My excursions into the garden and local area enabled my colleting. I had no qualms about gathering creatures or items. I coveted them and believed it was my right to do so. To take possession of my environment and everything within it.

tsee-tsee-tsee-tsee-chu-chu-chu

Curiosity fuelled my search for new things. I craved different colour snail shells, particularly the yellow and black swirled kind found in the wonderland of my grandma's garden. I gathered more and more. Kept every piece I found, fearful they would be lonely, that they needed the companionship of their fellows. Jars and tins filled with chaotic intensity. Overflowing like my overstimulated mind.

pee-chew, pee-chew, titcha-titcha

My grandad was a gardener, with military rows of vegetables and beans, red-flowered and tufted topped. Leaves instead of a lawn. The rotavator would chug and turn heavy earth, dark and sweet-smelling. He was not a large man, but with strength and energy, he worked tirelessly. He had a full head of blonde grey hair and would pour the second cup of tea from the pot without a strainer. Saturated leaves dark in the golden liquid. I still refuse to drain a cup. The inside of his teapot was dark stained, and woe betides anyone who suggested it be scrubbed. He would send me out with a blue ice cream tub amongst the rows collecting caterpillars. To save them from the birds. They would be taken to the plat to other plants. The plat was an extension of his garden, leased from the council, a private allotment he had tended for decades. I collected as many as I could, from tiny new hatched babies to fat squashy beasts on the verge of pupating. I would present my spoils proudly for appraisal. Earth engrained hands would gently shake the tub, shuffling its contents. Hands that were always active with tools, or a home rolled cigarette which would dampen between his lips. Small tobacco threads escaping their fiery demise would be plucked away. Over the road to the plat he would go. Through a gate where I believed my butterfly haven was secreted. A Devonshire rainforest of colours dancing between greenery beyond the high hedge across the lane. He fed those caterpillars to the chickens. I was not told until after his death.

    Jars of skeletal stick insects and raisin like slugs were thrown out with startling regularity. But my precious box of butterfly wings was left intact. Pieces of birds' eggs on little cotton wool cradles remained in their shoebox, feathers kept in bundles, sorted to size and colour. Birds' nests protected by toilet paper, perfectly woven with soft lined cups, a safe space to raise gaped mouthed babies with tiny darting tongues. My prized nest contained hairs from our spaniel Ringo who malted profusely. When Ringo died we buried him under the apple tree in Bumbles garden alongside Danny, my uncles King Charles spaniel. When Grandad Bumble died Bumble moved and the new owners bulldozed the garden.

    Gone was the low hedge where I would watch Robins nesting, the rose garden where long thorns grabbed at bare legged visitors who wanted to inhale their scent.

The low stone wall harboured slow worms and yellow shelled snails. It took a lot of convincing for me not to go digging under the vacated roots to recover the remains of my childhood friends who had been unceremoniously evicted. I wasn't allowed anything bony inside. Skulls of birds that were killed by the cat were not permitted. Nor those of rodents. Pets that inevitably died were buried and on no uncertain terms was I allowed to dig them up for their beautiful little skulls. I had a guinea pig that lived indoors. It had beautiful long hair and was coloured like a tortoiseshell cat. She died on Christmas Day, and because of the driving rain was not buried. Instead, she was wrapped up in a towel and sealed in a Ziploc bag and deposited in the freezer. When spring came, and the ground softened I took her back out and she was perfect. But I still had to relinquish her to the ground.

    Mere fragments remain from my early gatherings. Each is beautiful, not only for itself but for the history of them. I remain fascinated by them. Beauty is not a visual state. They feel beautiful when held. Smell a certain way, evoking snapshots of times filed away in memory. Time capsules opening paths to other destinations.

    A variety of frames meander up the staircase wall. None match. They are not spaced accurately. Instead, a tumble of magnolia margins acts as a banal backdrop. They are not a narrative. There is no family path, events unmoving with bad hair and awful jumpers. Embarrassed posing waiting for the film to be developed. Did I keep my eyes open despite the flash? Singular stories, photograph moments jostle up against a car boot sale print, postcard, mediocre watercolour. Pockets of joy in a stairwell only I use. Items repurposed. Chipped plaster bust where my glasses sit redundant as I refuse to wear them. A moleskin top hat, a small solid bowler, and felt trilby mark the entry to my study. A space of no distinction with a door that refuses to stay open.   My grandma had a large conch shell with a sun-bleached spikey exterior and perfect spiral pyramid. It was chipped in places allowing the porcelain inside layers to peek through. The underside was so smooth it was soft, cold and salmon pink as if it was lined with rose petals. The colour darkened as it retreated deep inside. I would listen to the sea, pressing the coldness to my cheek using both hands to cradle its weight.

kaswooosh, kaswosh, tikatikatikatika, plinkplininkink, shwosh

She also had a nautilus shell. Orange and cream with a gentle rippling surface. It was intricately carved with patterns encircling a hand holding flowers. Tiny tools grasped by a sailor had worked away the outer layers to reveal the iridescence beneath. I was not allowed to listen to the sea from this shell, it was too delicate, and I too clumsy. I inherited the nautilus, but the conch disappeared. I love the nautilus, it resides upon a shelf alongside a picture of a girl in a blue dress, made entirely of butterfly wings, and a Victorian mechanical bird with real feathers. He sings in his gilded cage and osculates at the turn of a key.

bee-beebee-bee, bee-bee-bee, beeeeee, bee-bee-bee, bee-bee-bee, pippippippip-bee ticaticaticatica

There is also a nautilus I collected from Cape Tribulation, Australia, a large brown seed from a beach in New Zealand, and shells kept in pockets from all over the world. All beautiful with memories. But I really would have liked the conch shell. Not only for the sea but because it made an excellent doorstop.

My attachment to this bundle of items I cannot fathom. Singularly they are all different. Each has its own story to tell, a path that leads to the same resting point. Recently I was gifted a brooch made with a butterfly wing.

The blue luminous behind a sheen of glass. Each small powdered scale magnified.

    My collection has been cultivated over my life. It is not a throwaway novelty. Now is the time of instant gratification, the newest fad, the latest fashion. I seek the curiosity cabinet historically curated. Spark conversation, ignite wonder. It graces my home. Less reckless and ferocious. Discerning choices that have made it through the many relocations and times in storage. I add a collection of experiences that lead me far from a Devonshire garden. Fairy-wrens chittering amongst the foliage. The silence that surrounds only you in the rainforest, whilst a symphony continues ten feet away. I have framed passport pages, not as proof, but because the stamps and visas are beautiful. Tiny masterpieces of block ink and biro handwriting. The world has opened up, massive and waiting. Yet it feels lesser than my childhood boundaries. It is more accessible than the other side of the railway bank used to be. As I wander over different paths I gather pockets of treasure. I remain the girl with an ice cream tub and scabby knees. On her own. Cataloguing her latest boon. Imagining what else there is to discover.

Sunrise to the Sound of Bubbles

My vet has a wonderful Eastern European accent.
 Can you hear the bubbling?
 Her breath was laboured. Sides heaved with the effort. Inhale. Exhale. Inhale.
 Crackles surged up through the stethoscope as I was given a guided tour of her lungs.
 I listened to the bubbling and her talking. Drug options. Financial implications. Realistic outcomes.
 We can take care of everything. Enjoy her. It is better for her to go before she is distressed.
 Can you cut her head off?
 Disbelief flashes across her face. Eyes widen beneath the thermal-lined hat. Protection against the crisp January morning.
 Cut her head off?
 I want to keep it. Mount it.
 Gloved fingers snap shut the clips on her toolbox.
 Shook her head.
 No. I will not cut her head off.

Dead Zoo

I stood transfixed, drawn into the eyes of the animal before me. Close enough to see each retractable claw nestled in peach coloured fur on enormous paws. I step closer. Press my hand to the glass. My breath mists up the surface. I wipe it away. Its face is level with my own. Poised. Alert. Black liquorice lace lips pulled back displaying pointed off white teeth.

Reflections move around me as people pass through. Shoes clip on polished floorboards worn lighter by the paths of a thousand footsteps. Ghosts flicker across the glass as they meander within caves of wonder.

The Royal Albert Memorial Museum (RAMM) in Exeter is a treasure trove. Collections gathered over generations are on display. It is similar to museums across the world, except it houses one of my favourite things. Recently it was refurbished, and as I walked upon the familiar floorboards I was astounded at how beautiful the alterations are. It was new and exciting, it didn't smell of dust. With refurbishment comes choices, what should remain on display, and what should not. As I journeyed through the provincial exhibits I began to wonder if my favourite had been deemed worthy. As I progressed panic began to rise. Gone were the rooms filled floor to ceiling with individual cases of specimens. the individual capsules containing a dead zoo had been opened. Remounted, freed from the isolation they now were resplendent in airy bright displays. Animated and vibrant they reflect their previous living states. Yet they weren't all here. The displays allowed for space and circulation, the opportunity to fully appreciate the exhibits. Not all the collection could be accommodated.

He had not been sacrificed. He was exactly as he should be. I revisited the details of the hairs flowing over the crown of his head, tufting atop white fringed ears. His colours ripple, burnt orange, black, pale creams and golds. There is time to look. All the time in the world.

This tiger has historical significance.

George V ascension to Emperor of India and his subsequent visit in 1911 would not have been complete without a large-scale hunt. His role as the head of the British empire entitled him to prestigious hunts and enabled him to flaunt his prowess and strength not only as a man but as the colonial ruler. Only a tiger hunt would do, and his subjects would benefit from the spoils.

Tiger hunting was not an invention of the British Raj. Elite safaris date to the early 16th century, rising from Mughal emperors. The tradition grew in popularity until the dynasty fell in 1857. Big game hunting became a favourite pastime for the elite British Raj and underpinned stereotypical assumptions regarding their rights to rule. Hunts showcased their royalty, power, wealth, and masculinity. Wildlife was eradicated. Tigers were the ultimate trophy and were targeted with reckless abandon. Historically shooting tigers had been a coming-of-age ritual for young Indian Princes, under British rule it was the right of the colonists. Everything was a commodity within the colonies. A crop to be reaped by those in power. The cats were vilified as 'terrible bloodthirsty beasts with an unquenchable desire for human flesh.' therefore legitimising the slaughter. Exeter's tiger is a 'beautiful though ferocious animal'. Proud and upstanding surrounded by foliage reminiscent of is a natural environment. He was mounted by Rowland Ward who specialised in realistic renderings of exotic animals. Wards premises resided in Piccadilly and was affectionately nicknamed 'The Jungle'. Their creations varied from Queen Victoria's pet dogs to Percy Cowell-Cottons elephant, which reputedly had the second-largest tusks on record. Unsurprisingly, the cost of Exeter's tiger reflects the quality and speciality of workmanship. The cost of the mount plus extensive alterations to the RAMM was met by Sir Channing Wills. The total cost exceeding £24,000 today. Wills generosity was not unnoticed, and the tiger was unveiled amidst much pomposity and was widely publicised; His Majesty's prowess with the gun in the hunting of big game during his stay in India will be fresh in the public memory. It has been made familiar by the remarkable series of moving pictures of the scenes which have been shown in all parts of the British Isles. His Majesty secured a very large number of trophies, which he decided last year to distribute among certain museums of the country. Eight tiger skins were presented to these institutions, four of them being allotted to the national museums, London, Edinburgh, Cardiff and Dublin, and the others to the four provincial museums, namely, Exeter, Norwich, Leicester, and Bristol.

  A noble exhibit, he was the crowning jewel in the museums' collection. Over 100 years later I am still awestruck by this macabre gift.

  I met Bristol's' tiger by accident on a primary school trip. Lured into rooms on the promise of immortalised animals. I found a crouching tiger. His pelt was much lighter than his counterpart. Muted. His eyes a pale yellow, their surface seeming scratched and lacklustre.

With a furrowed brow and bared teeth, I felt this animal was scared. Frozen in fright at the sight of a rifle-wielding monarch atop an elephant. His last position rendered timeless within a mahogany case.

My fascination with taxidermy began amongst the cases in the RAMM. I spent hours counting the bugs and butterflies displayed like jewels in velvet-lined drawers. Domes of birds in flight nestled amongst the wood and glasshouses of mammals placed higgledy-piggledy at neck cricking heights. I sought taxidermy out. Within Caernarfon Castle, I discovered the museum of the Royal Welch Fusiliers and was instantly fascinated. Not with their illustrious history, or the beautifully curated displays of weaponry and uniforms, but with a large, albeit sparse glass case containing a goat. He stands proudly, his long brown coat combed and pristine, head held high, crowned with magnificent curling horns. Wearing a white halter which was pointlessly tied to a ring, just in case of escape. He has a shiny shield on his forehead which distorts the reflections of overly inquisitive children. He was beautiful, and as I observed him I wondered why some animals got preserved whilst others did not. What about all the other goats that stood alongside the soldiers in sepia-toned photographs in the museum? Many were more handsome and impressive with long white coats wearing blankets resplendent with golden embroidery. Why were they not worthy of immortalisation?

I understood the significance and reasoning behind my tiger. He was a gift from a gun-toting king. Killed to educate, a display for study and enjoyment. A trophy proving the king's prowess and rule over a huge empire, a relic from the raj. The more taxidermy I saw, made with varying skill I questioned were these the best examples of each species? Is that why they had been preserved in this way?

The desire of hunters to bag themselves large

trophies spelt carnage for the natural world, especially the colonies. Here the wealth and assets of the country were available for harvest and exploitation by their ruling powers. Game was a commodity. A prize. Taxidermy enabled display and a public show of power and ownership as well as for scientific interest. In America Bison were hunted to the brink of extinction, Africa saw its enormous herds dwindle and across Asia species once common disappeared. Hunters were seduced by the guaranteed premier trophies advertised by travel agencies, and they killed regardless of need or want. Seeking something grander, larger, more beautiful. Nonchalance regarding the animals was commonplace as the elite basked in lands of endless abundance. Uncountable numbers were killed and discarded. As taxidermy rose in fashion it made its way into the home. It became an accessory, and every well to do Victorian lady sported an example of a dead creature, whether it be a bird upon a hat, a fur swept around shoulders or adornment carved from a tortoiseshell. The variety and creativity are astounding. Home became decorated with antlers and skulls, singular mounts and entire scenes graced hallways and mantlepieces. Elephant foot umbrella stands, and coal buckets, gold-tipped tusks, novelty and curiosity items, Wards notorious grizzly bear dumb waiter. These were not museum exhibits or scientific specimens, and purely ornamental. And like most fashions, it passed. However, collections remained and were added to.

    When visiting museums and historical properties I am struck by the presence of at least one tiger skin. Open mouth with a garish pink false tongue and surprised stare. Its pelt flattened and prostrate as if it has fallen victim to an ACME steamroller. Its inclusion part of the ancient pile checklist.

    * crumbling romanticised areas of masonry – check.
    *creepy portraits- check.

*velvet ropes- check.
*dead things that indicate our position in historical aristocracy.
*a showcase of our power over all that we own.
*proof of our ability with weapons and our philanthropy that we share these prizes with guests.
*also, we are rich and can afford to travel.

With the number of animals killed, I am surprised there are not more of them draped about. According to historical Mahesh Rangarajan 'over 80,000 tigers…were slaughtered in 50 years from 1875-1925. But it is possible that this a fraction of the numbers actually slain.' The immediate effect was the loss of the largest and strongest individuals from the gene pool. This was notable amongst African elephants as large tuskers are virtually extinct.

After WW1 a significant shift in global attitudes towards the natural world caused an alteration in the perception of big game hunting. As colonialism began to fall the conservation movement started to gain pace, yet initially had little impact. Post-colonial hunting in India skyrocketed until 1971 when tiger hunting was banned despite huge protest at the economic fallout. In 1975 Kenya followed suit banning trophy hunting. The notion of killing and preserving animals for sport was an affront to the spirit of the age. Taxidermy fell from fashion in the late 20th Century as people became aware of the plight of the natural world and humanities impact. It was a relic of a time of ignorance and abundance. The French natural history museum has an exhibition dedicated to species either extinct of rear extinction. Some are too precious to display, such as the sole specimen of a black emu skeleton. Yet many institutions have liquidated their collections, considering them a reminder of colonialism, outdated and against conservationism. In 1996 Eton college asked Bonham's to 'dispose of the bulk' of its collection as it was 'irrelevent to the needs and interests of present-day schoolboys.' St Michaels Mount in Cornwall auctioned its collection, and although it was not of vast value it was a collection of 'historical and scientific importance within the context of its surroundings.' Not only were the animals lost to nature, but their preserved forms were also being disposed of permanently.

There had been a resurgence in taxidermy as an art form and many early examples have been resurrected from storage. Damien Hirst is prolific in using animals in his work. Personally, I cannot define it as art, but everyone is entitled to their opinion. Hirst, himself a taxidermy enthusiast tried to purchase the entirety of Walter Potters whimsical collection. Potter created whimsical pieces, scenes of schools, circuses, and the famous 'Kittens Wedding' which was shown in the V&A as part of The Victorian Vision display in 2001. Potters' collection was eventually housed in The Jamaica Inn, Cornwall, where economic considerations forced it to be auctioned in 2003. Hirst offered £1m for the collection, which was rejected by Bonhams. The sale made a little over £500,000, and the collection was split. Yet the coverage it was given indicates there is still macabre curiosity with the form. Recently the Fox's Glacier Mint polar bears were auctioned. Once a powerful advertising tool that toured the country, they are now pieces of interior design. Decorative non-functioning furnishings.

As I discovered more examples of taxidermy, I found that the variety of pieces varied as much as the reasons for their preservation. Creatures of notable merit were often celebrated by being stuffed and displayed for all to see, or at least parts of them. Racehorses often had their hooves removed (after death) and made into inkwells or jewellery boxes. I knew a lady who owned such an item, except this was the hoof of her favourite pony. Inside the lid was a small glass pocket enclosing some of its hair. She had polished it until the silver plate had worn away and recounted stories of her youth when she was wild and free across the Devon countryside. She didn't own a single photograph of her pony, but she kept its hoof by her bedside and in it kept trinkets and elastic bands. She wanted to be buried with her trinket box because she was afraid it would be thrown away, it meant nothing to anybody else.

Hunting became a way for British colonialists to show masculine self-identity, over local society and fellow countrymen, an identity which was then articulated with triumphant rhetoric. Hemmingway was an avid trophy hunter and is included in Ward's record of hunters *Records of Big Game*. In his account *The Green Hills of Africa* (1935) he considers the dominance of the white male hunter over all other beings.

I was thinking about the bull and wishing to God I had never hit him. Now I had wounded him and lost him [...] Tonight he would die, and the hyenas would eat him, or worse, they would get him before he died. [...] I did not mind killing anything, any animal, if I killed it cleanly, they all had to die and my interference with the nightly and seasonal killing that went on all the time was very minute, [...] But I felt rotten sick over this Sable bull. Besides, I had wanted him, I wanted him damned badly...

The arrogance shown here is typical of the time, yet there is apathy towards the demise of the bull. In later writing Hemmingway's view of trophy hunting altered, as with many others toward repentance. However, hunting continues to be economically huge in Africa. Postcolonialism has enabled widespread commercial exploitation with revenue at an estimated $132-$436 million annually. The figures being so broad due to the lack of accurate records and amounts being siphoned into corruption and criminal activities. Rowland Ward as a company continues to trade as a trophy hunting facilitator in South Africa. It advertises its historical credentials referring to 'The Jungle' and Wards' expertise in mounting trophies. These companies claim they aid conservation efforts, protecting species, ensuring there is a population to hunt. It seems there is still a market for command over the colonial environment and everything in it.

New taxidermy is making its way into our museums for various reasons. Mainly it is to preserve aspects of our dwindling natural world. Cardiff museum is not only home to another of George V tigers. But also, a contemporary mount. A Sumatran tiger called Bryn spent his life at the Welsh Mountain Zoo. His life was spent as a key exhibit for the zoo, not only because he was spectacular, but also in raising awareness of the plight of the Sumatran tiger. He died of natural causes and now will continue this work in a different residence. The Sumatran tiger is critically endangered, and unfortunately soon the only examples are likely to be of a similar ilk to Bryn. He will be catalogued along with the Tasmanian Tiger, the Dodo, Passenger Pidgeon, and Lonesome George. Lonesome George was the only survivor of a giant tortoise of his species, rediscovered from extinction in 1971 in the Galapagos. He was known as the world's rarest creature in his last years and was relocated to the Charles Darwin Research Station for his protection. His death in 2012 was the end of the species and his remains were preserved. George is displayed in an exhibit dedicated to him at the research station where he died and serves as an important symbol for conservation efforts in the Galapagos. Like most animals that are either extinct or facing extinction due to human activity. Lonesome George served to illustrate this and people acted. The goat population which had decimated tortoise habitat were eradicated and in 2003 Pinta island was declared goat free. Project Pinta seeks to restore the island, including its giant tortoise population. Using taxidermy as a tool to highlight extinction as well as educate about those we have lost has created a resurgence in popularity and practice.

However, controversy continues. Animals have often been gifted between countries as signs of friendship and cooperation. Akin to the days of colonialism animals remain chattels and are symbolic of certain nations. In 1999 Hsing-Hsing, a giant Panda gifted to America from China died. It is currently illegal to taxidermy a Panda. Afraid of offending to China-US authorities were unsure of what to do with Hsing-Hsing, and so put her into storage at the Smithsonian until a decision could be made. Pandas are the global emblem for conservation and extinction, yet unlike the Sumatran tiger and Lonesome George they cannot be displayed posthumously as an example of what is at risk. In 2003 Ken Walker exhibited a panda at the World Taxidermy Championships. Walker used Hsing-Hsing as inspiration and rendered a mount so convincing, he had to prove it was not authentic. Ironic to think the most realistic panda mount created is a forgery. There is a growing market for extinct creatures to exhibit, and taxidermists are using their skills to create such pieces. Recently Singapore commissioned a Dodo. Surprisingly there a few examples of this bird as skeletons and skins were lost as they were seen more as a food source rather than of scientific relevance.

    The refurbishment of the RAMM, the investment in new exhibits and the continued popularity of natural history museums worldwide indicate an awareness of our world that was not present at the birth of taxidermy. Now extinct creatures are being joined quickly by others. However new pieces are bringing new knowledge that our forebears did not have. Instead of kings who can kill tigers for their subjects, we want those who can protect.

    I am enthralled by taxidermy because it bridges the chasm between life and death. What we decide to keep and what we discard.

Evelyn

I have perfected the art of detachment. Allowing my body to go through whatever trial is was subjected to whilst my mind takes itself away to safety and birdsong. I would picture the sky, duck egg blue, curved and dimpled, awash with swathing clouds. Listen for the sounds of fast-flowing water tripping over stones and the far-off monotonous burr of tractors. There is always birdsong.

The body is an amazing machine, and mine, though horribly flawed still recognised the mechanics of childbirth. Artificially created and early. Induced hypodermically and accompanied by invasive explorations which both terminated, and butchered, the abnormal invalid foetus swaddled within my defective womb.

Convulsions swept my body. Numb and automatic. A white sheet cut me in two, a barrier against what was happening. Figures in white with masks and judgemental eyes went about their business. Alone and ashamed, encased in this private facility I learnt the reality that I would not become a parent. Here was the consequence of my inability, and the decision that I could not bear, the thought of carrying a child that would not live. To become attached, form an emotional bond that couldn't blossom. To watch my belly grow. To undulate with weirdness as my little parasite became real, proving life was there.

I lay being prodded and poked. Unfeeling. Invaded and emptied. They left me to get dressed. The tiny body I had expelled was nowhere. I knew it had tiny fingers and a face. I saw it on the pre-procedure scan in a blurry monochrome bubble. An erratic heartbeat, disfigured form, multiple abnormalities. But she had been mine.

I waited in the shiny off-white box. Artificial lights. Wipe clean furnishings. Waiting for it to be brought back. This child I would live without, but, however invalid had been real. Just waiting to say I was sorry. That I had let it down, I couldn't perform the function women were meant to fulfil.

After forty minutes I crept to the reception. A huge sanitary towel a cumbersome brick in my jeans. To the woman, also in white, with a fake smile and customer service voice. The painkillers wearing off.

The foetus had been disposed of as medical waste. She confirmed my billing address. She called me a taxi.

Whole House

I talk to the walls. To the mirrors. To my reflection in the windows when it's dark and I leave the curtains open. Someone could look in and reply and we will stare in a silent pantomime.

The whole house of stone walls rough to my lips, puckered, grey lintel over the fireplace. Catch an eye watching from the recess of a spoon. Filigree handle, shallow dished and dented. Fantasise over building a fire. Watch flames lick the logs like a greedy child at ice cream. Dust, the ashen remains. A powdered shadow of brightness. Grey masks grace the mantle clock. Monotonous timepiece black hands sliding across the ivory moon.

I whisper. To the walls hoping the sound goes through. The neighbours will recognise my voice. They know when I am silent. Whisper to the vent in the kitchen where the stone is thin. Sing loudly. Words fill the air. Empty echoes.

I could get a cat, but I'm no-ones butler. I could get a dog, but I don't like walking in the rain. From eyes flow unseen tears. But the joy of frosty mornings, grass snapping beneath your wellingtons, the tart smell of cold, and the mist that glides along the rivers surface, that flowing veil, is almost enough it tempt me. Then I remember the signs 'pick up after your dog'. Romance. Tied up in a plastic shroud.

I am in the whole house. A whole house with only half the contents. This is what I have become when you become half a couple. Half everything in the hope another half will join you and the crockery may match.

My stone barrier hard and safe, where within I am vulnerable in my softness. Bubble wrap around my broken heart. Duct tape across window pane's cracked spiderweb. Space too small for two. But they will come. Stilted phrases haphazardly glued to making patchwork conversation. More fish in the sea.

I don't want a fish. Gawping eyes, pouting lips, cold moist kisses disturbing the surface of the water.

Hazy softness blurring features as a shaft of sunlight illuminates the dancing dust pirouetting an inch above a thickly piled rug. Hang tarnished mirrors through the hallway, murky reflection distorted when I pass. Each holds its own forgotten face. Look to the half-remembered shapes in the walls. Sometimes we race through the frames. Gilt trapped. Silver-less patches spreading like mould across antique glass. Just parts of me. Pieced together. Make a whole.

Becoming Fantastic

I have been an addict since childhood. Colouring in the faded lines that decorated my grandads' forearm. A trinket from RAF national service. Which he hated. Green tinted outlines of a design picked from a wall, made by needles swilled in water after their previous journey into human skin. I would draw felt-tipped flowers all over my body. Transform my childish flesh into the fantastic. And I wanted them. My uncle had three. A dragon, a panther and a rose. My mother wanted butterflies on her thighs. Her brother told her 'Lovie, with thighs like yours they'd look like bats.' She got smaller butterflies, not smaller thighs.

At 18 I had a postage-stamp-sized butterfly etched into my stomach. Expansive around a coloured speck. I hoped that it would help make it beautiful. That I could own my body which I abhor. That I could accept it because I chose this. I wanted this here because it deserves decoration. I forget it's there now. When I catch it peeking at me in the mirror, momentary panic – cancer- no, I put that there. And I continued to draw all over my body.

I would sit for hours, just watching. Soaking in the atmosphere. Listening intently, hoping to catch the half secret behind the art. Days spent with a sketchbook perched on my lap in the corner. Scribbling away at traditional motifs. When starting a drawing of a koi essentially you sketch a rudimentary penis. I have pages of two-minute phallus waiting to be scaled into fish.

    The setup, my set up has become a meditation. Setting up for others, my practice. As individuals, we are so different when faced with the same task. Personal needs paving the way for alternative paths to the same destination. I use too much foil. Swooshes off the roll with a gleaming flourish. Stuck down to scratched steel with Dettol. Smooth out any creases with gloved palms to make a metallic savannah on which to build. It's almost a ritual, a precursor to the main event. This is where I still get nervous. The build-up. The waiting. The need to appear calm. Confident in my ability when inside I'm terrified of that first fatal mistake.

    The performance of preparation was mastered before I ever stepped onto the stage. I was intoxicated by the smell as soon as I entered the room. Clean taste hits the back of my throat. I am thrown back into the cloudy bath, run each time I grazed a knee or got caught by brambles when exploring the train bank. The shine from the surfaces gleams under excessive lighting, equipment within reach. Accessible. Waiting. Set up. 18RS in the Black Rat. 7RL in the Mickey Sharpz. Stencil the design on the chair. Clients in at 4. Follow instruction. Repeat back the groupings. Snap elastic bands over the needle bars and press the armature down. Check the depth proud from the tip. Never run or adjust another artist's machines. Just check the depth. Stencil clear strong lines. Blueprint skeleton. Simple Celtic knotwork. Easy to confuse, to make mistakes. All becomes clear with the shading. Until then a maze of lines. I track it with my finger, ensuring its continuous. Cut it from the sheet and leave it waiting. Double-check and step away. Remove clinging gloves. Powder washes away but the smell remains. Medical latex dries out my hands desensitises my fingertips. Makes me itch.

Glove up. Sit down. This one's yours.

Those three phrases are the best body purging trigger I have ever experienced. I pulled on professional and sat down.

But this was not my set up. Not my station. Not my machines. I was the wrong way around. The joy of being an awkward left-hander had taught me to work on the other side, so as not to drag my clip cord across my body, back and forth to the slab of pigskin, kindly donated by confused butchers.

Deep breath. Let's wing it.

Have you ever put something completely alien into another person's skin? Consider the act. That you are purposely scarring another human being. And they are willing. You both know it will be potentially painful that it can take a long time. Yet here they are. Under your hands, as you hope you remember what to do.

Mechanical process. Skin prep, stencil, Vaseline, machine and go. So simple. Who's worried? Settle into my hand. Inanimate. The shrill voice of the Sharpz erupts. The wrist is pliable. The skin running up the inner forearm is softer than the outer. Smooth, elastic, and surprisingly curved. Lines distort as the skin is pulled tight allowing the needles to penetrate. Minimal bounce. Lessens the risk of tearing. Don't press, don't go deep. Slowly track lines and breathe. The first wipes away. Recheck machine, voltage, throw. Go again. It's there forever. That first line of my first tattoo. My first client. I peeped my toe over the threshold of the world I wanted to frolic in. To announce my arrival and beg for admittance.

The first line is always the worst. The further in you get the fluidity comes. I was lost in this design. A 3'' square patch of person. Robotic. Ink, wipe, Vaseline, work. Shade, flick up through the skin, fade it out. Here is where I needed to be. Drunk on Dettol scent and adrenaline. Ink spattering my foil landscape. My own Jackson Pollock to screw up and throw away. Clinical waste.

It took too long. My first. As I agonised over each movement. My hands screaming in pain unused to the weight and the angles gripped between amateur fingers. But as we finished and cleaned the freshly wounded surface we locked eyes with relief.

There's trust each time I set needle to skin. It's a silent contract. I will try to realise what you desire. I shall paint you into the fantastic.

My first, second and third tattoos all lie with the same body. They are never yours, you cannot claim them. These pieces you agonise over, replay in your mind. Those you showcase as proof you belong. They walk away. They age, change. Ultimately decay.

My first tattoo. Its wearer died too young. He was crushed by a car on his driveway. The jack gave way. He was a father, and each of his children were represented on his body. Sometime after his death I was tattooing the mother of his children. The conversation wanders when working. You are not only a tattooist but a counsellor, entertainer, listener. She would have liked to have kept the images he had etched into his skin. A truth that he had loved them. Something more real than photographs. He was beautiful. His art was beautiful. It was such a waste when it was turned to ash. Someone so colourful and alive reduced to grey.

Tattoos are transient, altering over time. They age with the wearer, and to some extent are ownerless. The artist may never see their creation again. The wearer may be unable to view the piece in person. Do those who view the tattoo get to claim it? Dedication designs, memorial tattoos, omens that signify membership, religion, fandom. The connotations are endless, as speculative as the reasons people have historically felt compelled to decorate themselves.

Through the age's humans have sought adornment

and communication. Seeking beauty and understanding. Cave paintings, carvings, earthworks. This desire turned inward early in human history.

In 1993 an archaeological dig in Siberia uncovered something remarkable. It has since become a source of fascination, speculation and controversy. From the permafrost of the Ukok Plateau, the remains of a young woman emerged into daylight. Like many remains found in the permafrost, she had been exceptionally well preserved. She was buried with an array of items indicating she was a figure of importance within her society. She was flanked by six horses, spiritual escorts to the next world, a Chinese mirror, coriander seeds and an amount of cannabis. Items relating to royalty and shamanism. She was accompanied by two male warriors. This woman was at the pinnacle of the Pazyryk social ladder. As remarkable as this gravesite was it did not compare with the Ukok princess at its centre. She was wearing intricate and exquisite tattoos. They made her fantastic.

Designs of mythical animals frolicked across her body. Horned beasts, birds, leopards, and fish. Animals of significance. Dynamic images specifically stylised and etched into the skin. Full sleeves of intricate work, painstaking hours under the hands of the artist. Fresh and crisp as the day they were wrought some 2500 years previously. The creatures are distinct and specific to ones found at the time, as well as mythical beasts. They narrate and deep understanding of the world which they lived in, that they interacted with and shared with neighbouring people. Similar images have been discovered adorning other remains, repeated in paintings and carvings. These perpetuated images allude to a language or common understanding. Animals graced the skin of individuals across Siberia, the Scythian civilisation united through art. A primitive form of the elaborate hieroglyphs prolific in Egypt. Scholars believe the Pazyryks' used the tattoos as a symbol of their social standing, their identity, belief system. As they aged they gathered more, and in death, they became a guide to the next world and a way to recognise each other once they arrived.

The Ukok princess is the oldest example of a tattooed female found. Yet tattooed mummies are not uncommon. Otzi, also recovered from the permafrost, sports simplistic designs. Egyptian mummies were adorned with body art. It is found across the globe in early human history, at a time where civilisations were scattered, isolated, ignorant of others practice. It has evolved from indigenous communities that have followed their desire to decorate their bodies using a variety of methods. Traditional Maori and Polynesian tattoos are executed with ivory or bone combs that tap ink into the skin. Some Nordic designs were created by stitching ink-soaked tread through the skin, leaving a dark deposit as it was pulled through. A track of its journey. Japanese tattoos were hand-poked with meticulous precision by skilled artists creating wonderous complicated images. Connotations surrounding tattoos vary. The historical cultural significance of tattooing has become partially lost to mainstream current fashions. Some aspects remain embedded within specific cultures; however, many have been appropriated worldwide.

Tattooing is currently more visible than it has ever been. There are worldwide conventions, mainstream tv shows, exhibits and literature. The rise of the celebrity artist has been fuelled by the celebrity wearers who are prominent influencers across multiple platforms. People are proud of their art. Those with heavy coverage have made a huge financial commitment in their pursuit of tattoos. It is art and we have become avid collectors and consumers. However, there remains varied reactions to tattoos that continue today, especially the tattooed woman. As a female tattooist, I was considered a novelty. Some were happy to have my work, others flatly refused to let me touch them.

Initially, my coverage was the source of surprise and negativity. I lowered the tone. Stigma has lifted as attitudes change.

Weirdly I still find hand and facial tattoos taboo. They are a huge step for the wearer. These are areas that cannot be hidden and socially still receive the most reactions. Yet the stigma surrounding these placements is lifting. I had been told as a child hand tattoos meant you would not get a good job. Career killers. Luckily my hand tattoos have never been seen in an unfavourable light. I have an L and R on my respective hands, a nod to my inability to know my left from right. They are not political, or reactionary or have any connotations except my frequency at getting hopelessly lost. I do not have heavy coverage. All my work is unfinished for a plethora of reasons. I wear a variety of styles, some colour, some black and grey. They were not all chosen by me, even though the majority were drawn by me. I have green jigsaw pieces on my heels, a diamond adorns the inside of my ring finger, hummingbirds and a gilt cage in full colour on my arm with black and grey keys on the inner forearm. I have plans for my back, my thighs, buttocks and chest. It is addictive, moreish, and time-consuming. They draw attention, good and bad. The process is incredible. Alien. A pleasurable pain that floods the body with endorphins and adrenaline. It has been linked to self-harm. A sensory overload of sound, smell, the iron taste of excitement explodes on your tongue. You think about the next one whilst the needles enter your skin.

Human skin is an exhibition space, valued, purchased and sought after. Some gift their skin to tattooists, yielding their bodies to the desires of the artist for a reduced fee, or with the promise they will surrender the work once deceased. Good work is a form of advertisement for an artist, as is the opportunity to create unhindered and showcase talent. Historically tattoos have been collected by criminologist's who have studied the designs, seeking codes within the work. This was prevalent in Russia and neighbouring nations where prison and crime-related tattoos communicated with others fluent in the fraternal codes. Japan was heavily influenced by criminality. Wearers were often flayed, removing the skin as a trophy and form of identification. The earliest evidence of Japanese tattooing is seen on clay figurines. In the third century, AD chronicles tell of me young and old with decorated bodies and faces. In the seventh century, Japanese tattoos fell from favour and were used as a form of punishment and associated with criminality, including the Yakuza. At the turn of the twentieth century the practise was outlawed, however, it remained popular especially amongst organised crime as a method of identification and determining allegiances. They also became a form of currency, a piece of art that could be collected and sold. It is highly prized and valuable art with the wearer a human canvas. In 1948 tattooing was decriminalised and the art form expanded.

    Tattoos are also a curiosity, especially those from indigenous communities. Mokomokai, tattooed heads from New Zealand, were exhibited across the globe, as were shrunken heads from South America. The tattooed lady at fairground and circus sideshows, isolated tribes from the remote wilderness. There is a sense of other about such exhibits which now sits uncomfortably in modern society. The fascination with tattoos had caused them to become a commodity. They are collectables both in life and death. The Medical Pathology Museum in Japan boasts a collection of 105 full-body tattoos. These bodysuits are preserved in different ways, some dried and flat, others are wet specimens, and some have been mounted like taxidermy. They are controversial and precious, access is carefully controlled and highly restricted. Yet they continue to acquire new specimens.

I attended a tattoo exhibition in Falmouth museum. A regional museum, it champions the history and culture of Cornwall, its mining heritage, its people. Upon entering the building there was a sense of modernity and expression in the space and light created in the spaces. The exhibit itself was separate from the main space due to the nature of the contents. It is illegal to be tattooed under the age of 18. Most studios do not allow entry to those below the threshold. Upon entering the exhibition space, I was met with a wall of latex forearms, complete with long flexible fingers and cuticle detailing. Each of these arms hung in orderly rows, regimented with equal space around them, alone but part of a bigger picture. They were startling, uncomfortable yet beautiful. Each was decorated by a different artist. Each was unique. A showcase. A capsule of art singularly rendered and amalgamated into this visual event.

    I marvelled at these hands. At the creative skill of the artists and how distinct each outcome was. It highlighted the endless possibilities of the body, the endless possibilities of tattoo as a medium, and how it is an art form as well as a personal expression. The exhibition also had small pieces of skin. Suspended fragments in slightly yellowish liquid. A throwback from a Victorian apothecary shop window, or gentleman's curiosity cabinet. There was a small sign saying there were human remains that some people may find disturbing. I have never seen one of these signs in an Egyptian exhibit, with an open sarcophagus displaying mummies. Surely, they are the same?

    Collecting tattooed skin is not unusual. There are collections worldwide and museums actively seek to expand their catalogue and cultivate new corpuses. The Welcome Collection in London had over 300 individual fragments, there are also collections in Lisbon, Paris and Krakow. Contemporary pieces are also finding their way into museums, viewed more as artwork rather than pieces of skin. Retired teacher Geoff Ostling has gifted his body to the Australian National Gallery. His skin will be posthumously removed, preserved and exhibited, including his face and genitalia. Ostling began to get tattooed at 42 and says he 'decided to get tattooed because he felt it helped him take possession of his body.' Ostling is taking ultimate possession and has strategically organised procedures for his flaying and funeral. Ostling claims his skin could fetch half a million dollars on the illegal market trafficking tattoos and considers his donation like donating organs. Yet the sensitivity of preserving and displaying the skin has created uncertainty around its eventual residence. If the gallery rejects the skin it could be offered to other institutions. The popularity of skin preservation has created a market for those who can facilitate it. the National Association for the Preservation of Skin Art in America facilitates the removal and preservation of body art, sending a kit to the mortuary to remove the designated area and halt its decomposition. Six months later the piece is returned, the loved one receiving a framed memento.

    Belgian artist Wim Delvoye is known for exhibiting taxidermy mounts of tattooed animals, notably pigs. In 1999 he began working upon the skin of live animals shocking animal rights groups and audiences. Delvoye states 'I show the world works of art that are so alive, they have to be vaccinated. It lives, it moves, it will die. Everything is real. There is a divided opinion. Animal rights groups argue the pigs are enduring unnecessary suffering and fear. Delvoye believes he is repurposing the pigs as living canvasses. There is a market, especially in China where the skins are highly valued. A single pig could fetch up to $70,000. In 2006 Delvoye tattooed the back of Tim Steiner. Steiner is contractually obligated to exhibit his tattoo three times a year and upon death, his skin is to be 'harvested' and sent to art collector and gallerist Rik Reinking. Reinking has the rights to exhibit and sell the work. The prospect of an individual selling their skin seems more acceptable than a man tattooing and selling the skin of a pig. Here is the reality of choice. As adults we decide to tattoo our bodies, we decide if we want them to be seen or not, we are then able to decide what happens to them post-death. With regards to ancient remains, they are viewed differently, as scientific artefacts rather than pieces of art. They are 'intellectual property and that we have the right to use them for exhibitions and to study them. we're not doing this out of curiosity but in the interests of science. The soul is somewhere else, and we are studying the remains.' Modern exhibits however run the risk of impacting the subject's family and friends. ancient remains have the advantage of emotional as well as familial distance. We did not have a record of these people pre-death; they had no impact upon our daily lives.

Human remains exhibits raise questions of choice and consent. Who can claim them? Who has ownership and responsibility? Ancient communities did not expect to be discovered, unearthed and taken on worldwide tours. They did not expect to be of specific scientific interest or curiosity. Significantly many subjects have been repatriated and removed from display, especially examples from indigenous groups. In an article about the Ukok Princess, Dr Eriknova explained to the Siberian Times in 2004.

She was a beautiful young woman, who they dug up, poured hot water and chemicals upon and subjugated to other experiments. They did this to a real person.

The reality of her is underpinned by a recreation of her face by taxidermist Marcel Nyffenegger. For over two weeks he painstakingly reconstructed her face from an exact model of her skull. The finished bust is adorned with a copy of her tattoos. Indeed, the tattoos are now so recognisable and appreciated they have returned to living canvasses. It has been named Scythian animal style art. Such is the influence and appreciation of the artistry and legend resurrected by this prehistoric woman. As these individuals sat down next to her artists set up I wonder did they consider the young woman 2500 years ago sitting with her artist undergoing her own evolution. Could she imagine the thwack of latex gloves being pulled on, the electric buzz of machine erupting into life? Ancient meets modern in a flawless scar. As Dr Polosmark explains 'I think we have not moved far from the Pazyryka in how the tattoos are made. It is still about a craving to make yourself as beautiful as possible.' To become fantastic.

Tea with Grandma Jean

Either side of the council issued mantlepiece is a small figurine. One, an elderly lady, hands clasped wearing a pinny. Hair pulled back in a bun. On the other side an old man with tartan slippers reclines in an armchair. They rest on small plinths. One says Grandma, the other Grampa. No one ever referred to my Grandfather as Grampa. He was Grandad Jean. Since he died we all take turns sitting in the chair opposite my Grandma.

It was different then. No one made a fuss. You just got on with it. I still had to go to work and look after the babies. I cleaned the big house for ten shillings and sixpence. The rent was ten shillings. I bought a packet of cigarettes once. Twopence. Just floated off and away. I thought well what was the point of that? I decided I'd be better off with a pound of apples.

Grandma Jean is softer with age. Arthritic hands knit with lightning speed. Little jumpers and hats for children in Moldova. The scraps of yarn she winds up and keeps in a bag in the back bedroom. She is not a small woman. Bosoms like barrage balloons are held up by structurally engineered bras that she methodically washes and hangs triumphantly on the line. White bunting gracing the garden path. Her hair is styled like the Queens and hasn't altered in my memory. At 86 she has little grey. She doesn't go far now. Not without either her walking stick or wheelie frame, complete with brakes and padded seat in case her legs start to buckle.

Grandma lost girls. She had four boys. But lost every girl.

One came late, it was dark. And Rod bundled it up in newspaper and put it in the fire. The ground was frozen. There wasn't much there...I wanted a girl. We thought Brian was a girl. He felt different. He came early. My own fault. Doing too much. We had just got the house on the Avenue, so I had to walk to The White Horse to get to Panters for curtain material. Got home and it was all measured wrong. I had to go all the way back to White Horse the next day. Did the curtains. But I'd lost a day then. I cleaned the new house. Moved everything, then cleaned the old house. I had to get back to work. He came early. Reckon he'd had enough. I'd done too much. He was ever so poorly. In an oxygen tank for a while. He went right back to four-pound six. They didn't have much hope for Brian. But I knew if I got him home I'd get him right. Now Raymond was an ugly baby. Came quick. He was all covered in this thick grey grease. I gave him to the midwife. Quite disgusted I was. I told her 'I thought we could do better than that.' But it all melted away and he went all pink. Pretty little thing then. But I didn't grow much on him at the start.

She has a Devon accent that flows along, comfortable and slightly threadbare. Her world is not large. A walking distance circumference of stories and memories. We have heard them all. Over and over. Tales that have become the bonds between us.

Mother had all girls. We would come downstairs and there would be another one. We didn't know she was expecting. She still worked...

It is accepted amongst the family that Nanny Gill was '*A bit of a flirt*'.

They didn't all live. She smothered one by accident. Fell asleep feeding her. We had gone under the table in case of bombs and mother fell asleep. She got in trouble for that one. Elsie Freda. I remember her. Nice little thing. Quiet. I remember she lost one, one day. We all had to look. Found it all folded with the blankets where she had stripped the bed...

Her tone doesn't change. Pragmatic. Sentimental. She smacked each of her sons before bed in case they had misbehaved in the day. She only got rid of her twin tub because they could no longer repair it. You never visit during Wimbledon. Racks of spoons gleam along the walls. Racks of chocolate tins in the kitchen contain rock buns and everyday biscuits. We drink tea and talk over the clickety-clack of needles darting away. When the scrap bag is full, I take it home to crochet colourful blankets.

Don't you settle Deelee. You're not suited. It would be like trying to cage the wind.

Rich In Shit

There is a widely held misconception that people with horses must have money. This is because the average cost of keeping a horse at grass livery is between £2,925 and £3,630 a year. In my experience horses are money pits. Giant hairy eating machines. Head, tail, leg at each corner and generally rampant flatulence. Maybe this says more about the individual horses I have chosen to spend my life with, but many horse owners I know will agree with me that this is the case. Horses have been an integral part of the structure of our society and civilisation for aeons. Beasts of burden, transport, pleasure pursuits and status symbols. They powered agriculture, industry and war. They remain symbolic to many aspects of popular culture; there is still the mounted cavalry, the trooping of the colour, equine sports. But what about us? The Joe Bloggs horse owners fell in love with the concept of ponies while young and incredibly naive. Saturday's, doe-eyed at the riding school with clean jodhpurs and coloured wellies. Bless those children, little did they know.

Horses do not bring the glamour we watch avidly in the rarely televised events. Pristine animal and rider in perfect harmony. Exquisitely turned out acing a dressage test or getting that elusive clear round. Smooth lawns pre-first chukka, tea dresses and champagne amongst the huge horse boxes and long leather boots. They (in my experience) are distant and unreachable dreams.

Instead of the sleek and shining steeds, I adored, my first pony purchase was a Dartmoor foal. Direct from the moor at Chagford pony sale. £16.50. Scrawny, shivering and utterly wild. 'Max' became the centre of my world. After a few injuries and the bribery of many carrots and polos (essentials in the pony owners arsenal), he succumbed to my attention. This pony was walked and fussed, adored. Quintessential Dartmoor, small strong, patient, with an intelligent gleam in his eyes and tiny ears that became spherical when he grew his winter coat. This fantastic fur that waterproofed and insulated his little body. I always felt his fur was made of three layers. Short furry mole-like hair close to the skin, a thermal layer. Then a fluffy air trapping one, like an Arran jumper, knitted by your Grandma and wheeled out each autumn. Finally, long hair to direct rain across the body and drip away. Water never reached the skin or underlying fluff. The long hair curls and twists into tight spirals like a cartoon sheep. Hours spent nose deep in this coat, whispering secrets into those tiny pom-pom ears. Sadly, I grew, 'Max' did not.

A string of in-between ponies came and went. Always with problems. If it was crazy, dangerous, ugly or headed for the meat man it somehow ended up in our field. We boasted a collection of unwanted problem ponies. Luckily, by pure coincidence, my family ended up living in a house belonging to a company specialising in artificial insemination for cattle. The company had closed, and we secured the house, field and buildings for ridiculously low rent, so the fluctuating pony population was not a problem. Unfortunately, it came with an equally ridiculous name; Number 2 Cottage, Genus Insemination Plant. This soon became 2 Genus Cottage. Said luck ended as the property was put under compulsory purchase to build the new A30 near Exeter airport. It was demolished and concreted. We moved, and horses departed from the forefront of my life for many years. Then at 21, I decided that one of the holes in my life was horse-shaped.

The search for a new horse is stressful. Elimination processes are needed and must be brutal. Luckily, I had a vague idea of what I wanted, but above all, it needed to be chunky. No rider wants to consider 'does my bum look big on this. The other essential was can I get on from the floor? Which equates to not being too big and is willing to stand still whilst I flail about trying to get on. Ideally mounting from the ground would not be necessary, but everyone falls off. I opt for falling when it is more difficult to try and stay on, when you're past that point of no return and there is a little more dignity in hitting the ground; its best to admit defeat. There is an art to falling that I do not possess. Some riders glide to the floor and arise appearing unscathed to return to their politely waiting animal and they carry on. Lucky buggers. I seem to fall into the mud, or water, or some other non-descript effluent that clogs my nostrils and causes involuntary urging. Then generally I must try and catch my pony who has decided this is all a wonderful adventure and proceeds to disappear. Once caught it then decides it wants no further part in this tomfoolery and makes remounting a comedic affair. The rule is to always get back on. A mantra instilled by my mother, who coincidentally found these psychopaths for me to ride in the first place. Getting back on is the last thing you want to do when your pony is off auditioning for rodeo championships. Some have a dark twisted sense of humour dump their riders purely for sport. 'Dandy' was such a comedian. Probably the prettiest pony I had. A 13.2 strawberry roan Welsh section D. His coat in summer would change to a deep speckled peach, darkening around his ears and ankles. Well-mannered and affectionate until you got on. His repartee was astounding. Vertical buck, from a standstill, drop and roll, shoulder throws, tight and unexpected spins. This was a pony wasted on countryside hacks, he had ambitions of becoming a world-class wrestler with his moves. Eventually, even my mother admitted defeat and classed him dangerous. My princess pink pony was 'sent on' after I made quite a dramatic contact with a windscreen. Bleeding and slightly broken my mother ever faithful to the mantra chucked me back on. I digress.

Mostly I was wanting that elusive something. That connection, the spark that indicates the start of a partnership. I wasn't looking for a horse, I was looking for *my* horse. I had been sold that romanticised ideal that out there somewhere was 'the horse'. I had been seduced by fantasy, I wanted the relationship portrayed in *War Horse,* my very own 'Joey'. The partnerships and glamour Jilly Cooper created in *Riders* and *Polo.* It also had to be a native breed.

For a small island nation, we have a vast diversity in our native horses. Each has different characteristics specific to their original location and needs of the breeders. Many of our native breeds have fallen out of fashion as their environment and place within the world has altered. Native horse and pony breeds are dwindling. On the critical list are the Cleveland Bay, Hackney, Dales, Suffolk Punch and Eriskay. Dartmoor and Exmoor are both endangered whilst Clydesdales, Fell and Highland are vulnerable the Shire and New Forest are also at risk. Most of these animals are fundamentally working horses. The carriage horses, draft horses, heavy horses. As machines took over their place within the world became obsolete.

As a child, my mother and I used to assist in showing heavy horses. Hours spent polishing brasses, oiling leather and intricately plaiting these giants with ribbons and flags. I loved the enormity of the Shires and

Clydesdales with their silken feather that dances when they walk, the gentleness and elegance combine with sheer strength and presence. There is nothing more awe-inspiring than watching a group of heavy's race. They thunder along, shovel-like hooves cutting into the earth with weighted power. It is a noise like no other, deep rhythmic and rumbling. Often these races are held as a feature at race meets, a novelty act between the more serious spectator sport. I have little time for the spindly prancing thoroughbreds, although I admire their athleticism, it is not a heavy, nor more specifically, a Suffolk Punch.

The Suffolk Punch is one of Britain's oldest breeds, its studbook was established in 1768. Distinguished by its deep chest, huge powerful haunches and relatively short legs. They are always chestnut in colour with no feather and minimal markings. They are also considered to be the rarest horse in Britain. The Suffolk is smaller and stockier than their heavier counterparts, they have a large head and small eyes and shine like burnished copper. They are ideal agricultural animals, patient, strong, with legendary stamina. They are not bogged down in the mud by heavy feathering, are elegant enough to be versatile and less expensive to keep than the larger heavies. I adored them and was aware even then of their scarcity in the show ring. The decline of heavy horses is well documented. At the start of the twentieth century, there were 2.6 million across the British Isles. In 2017, 464 pedigree foals were registered to these three breeds combined. 25 being Suffolk's. This species is rarer than the giant panda, indeed with around 80 broodmares left in the UK experts predict the breed could become extinct by 2027. In some small way, I wanted to preserve a tiny pinch of national heritage and identity. To forge a small affiliation with the horsemen gone by and protect a species under threat.

I had that dream horse in my mind, but I couldn't manage the sheer size of the Suffolk and so landed on a

Fell and Dales pony. Native breed, endangered. Black, elegant headed, a bigger version of 'Max'. Instead, I saw, and out of pity bought 'Blossom'. A 14hh underweight mistreated 3-year-old cob mare. While the Irish Cob has a long history its studbook was not officially founded until 1998. The breed was developed by the Romani in the UK and Ireland to pull their wagons, hence they're recognised worldwide under the blanket term 'Gypsy horses'. It seemed fitting as diluted gypsy blood runs in my veins. This could work.

    She had been starved and neglected. Broken as a yearling she had not had chance to mature either physically or emotionally before being put to work. Circumstances meant she had been ignored for months and the result was a vacant depressed bag of bones. She looked like she had crawled out of Auschwitz. So filthy she was beige, with a matted feather, an overly large head and no spark of interest. She also had an overly large attitude and vicious streak when around food or men. For those who haven't been privileged enough to have a long relationship with an animal, it is difficult to grasp the impact they have on your life. They are more than a pet, they are an integral part of you, and that intensifies when they come from a place of abuse.

    After the first bout of injuries; kicks, crushes, bites, purposeful foot-stomping and well-aimed flatulence. I gave this animal six months else she was becoming a £750 can of Chappie. Blossom bloomed. Never the prettiest of Cobs she has quite a pleasant face now that she has grown into it. Dark brown eyes ringed with white hairs as if someone got overenthusiastic with eyeshadow. Long whisker type hairs protrude around her eyes and velvet muzzle, these assist with spacial awareness akin to a cat. They're generally trimmed for the show ring, but she isn't show quality. Bloss, for a piebald mare, is too white. Bright white like a burnished pearl. Not the most practical colour. Next time

I'm opting for brown, in shades of either mud or horse excrement. When wet, her skin is covered in small black spots like a Dalmatian, unfortunately, the black hairs never came through. She has an extraordinarily thick tail that needs regular soaking in DAZ to try and eliminate some of the muck that gets mushed into it.

As she recovered she grew, filled out and muscled up. Physically she was a great example of her type with a thick neck and large apple bum. She developed a personality and sense of humour. She learnt how to drink tea from a mug and will politely share an ice cream cone, most of the time. Unsuspecting children are fair game, easily distracted they fall victim to her charms and lose whatever sweet treat they had held in their clutches. She is not averse to cake, chocolate, pasties or bananas. Given the opportunity, she has been known to snaffle a bacon sandwich and beak into Tupperware to gorge herself on the contents. Desperately nosey she will nonchalantly put her long moustached face through open windows to greet startled occupants. She has a love for baby things, human or animal. She interacts gently, with patience and sensitivity that I would not have credited to a horse. Especially one who was so unpredictable at the start.

Nothing can ever prepare the new owner for the reality of ownership. Breaking ice on water butts, losing wellies in knee-deep mud and the inevitability that this mud will soon be cementing itself under your toenails. When your hands are so cold they're burning hot with pain. Chilblains, hay nets, rats, head torches, multiple escapes, tangled electric fences, magical disappearing hoof picks, the rug wrecker who obviously doesn't want to be warm or dry. Stables, the daily joy of shovelling away the large digested hay net that she has stomped into your beautifully arranged bed, urinated over and slept on. White horse plus stable stains…

The rewards outweigh the work, at least they do in

summer. However, then it's a minefield of midges, horseflies, sunburn, buttercup burn, new grass madness, laminitis risks and sudden overnight grass bellies. For most, horse ownership is done for pleasure. The freedom and peace of being out in the countryside. To enjoy the landscape and reconnect with the world. For me, this is meditation time. I slip the tether of being contactable. I value this time. Just me, Bloss and the countryside. The view of the world is different on horseback. Not only for the obvious reason that you're elevated and can now peer over hedges and watch the progress of crops and livestock stoically on the journey to maturity and harvest. Suddenly you become aware. Exposed. Vulnerable. This animal is bearing you because it chooses to. It has its own brain (whether it is engaged or not is another matter) and therefore is not wholly under your control. A horse may not be at all bothered by the looming HGV in the single-lane road. She may well lull you into a false sense of security as a troop of Lycra-clad cyclists whoosh by, all frantic legs, thinly clad bobbling buttocks and rampant competitiveness. No, it is the menacing terrifying horse eating plastic bag that incites terror a swift shift into reverse and unnecessary snorting. That pony swallowing puddle which she dances around, let alone the fortnightly invasion of wheelie bins. These mysterious containers of doom filled with dismembered pony parts are the stuff of nightmares. But only sometimes. Do not ever expect consistency with their irrational fears.

  The freedom and exposure to the countryside you get from riding allowed me to enjoy it from a wholly new perspective. I observed the hedgerows passing by, mindfully tracking their journey through the seasons. Watched wildlife who are unthreatened by a horse walking along. The surreal minutes when a fox trots all slender limbs, russet tones attentive ears alongside you on a farm track. Once I found a mole, black, with the softest fur so smooth it felt wet. Above ground they're vulnerable, and in the middle of the road, they're suicidal. I put it in my pocket (much to its confusion) and carried it to a safe place. No doubt far from its territory, but I had the right intentions. Aware of your surroundings a different map grows in your mind, one that highlights tracks and pathways that lead to hidden treasures, a fallen tree that's perfect to jump, a long gallop where you can stand in the stirrups, arms outstretched and whoop into the wind. It's a different emotional connection to the land only brought about by the relationship with my horse. I fell in love again with my local area and began to appreciate it deeply. One of my favourite rides was across Lamberts Castle, an iron age hill in Dorset. Owned by the National Trust since 1981 it has been a designated site of Special Scientific Interest because of its ecology, geology and archaeology. Ancient and ringed with trees it's the perfect strategic stronghold with a view of the Jurassic Coast and away inland. On a clear day, you can see all the way to Portland. Patchwork agricultural land undulates away, pockmarked by houses and farms. Wildflowers peek through the springy carpet-like grass, but it's not grass, nor moss. It's a congregation of many plants all stitched together underfoot and punctuated with animal droppings and tenacious gorse saplings. Through the kissing gate and into the woods where puddles never fully dry. They just crisp over purposely to thwart the unsuspecting wanderer. Mosaic leaves cast a yellow-green glow in the weak pre-summer sun and the smell of the earth rises heady and thick to mingle with the wisps of mist sliding two inches above the dew. The car park is never empty as people congregate to walk overeager dogs across the lattice of footpaths. To gaze out over the land. To feel small in an overwhelming landscape. Or simply to walk the dog impervious to their surroundings, hunched and insular. Buzzards call, their voices bouncing around open sky as they lazily wheel above, always watching below. This is where I come to pay homage. And get rewarded for the trials.

There is nothing quite like the pungent fermented stench of concentrated mare piss at 6 am to make you question your sanity. Then, if you're extremely lucky you have an uneven stable floor, with a large depression perfect for collecting this stinking liquid. If you're even luckier this is where two rubber stable mats meet, and if stood on incorrectly squirts a spout of urine skyward. The icing on the cake comes when you're running late and rush to feed the wonderful not moody at all mare before going on date night. Picture it. Nice hair, dress, make up. Don't bother putting on overalls or wellies. And she knows, oh she knows. So, she pushes you off balance, step, squelch and yep…horse piss up the leg. I am thankful that my boyfriend has no sense of smell, the rest of the cinema is not my problem.

Blossom is newly retired. She is around 20 years old, which isn't a great age. But due to her early start and long working life, she has developed arthritis, a bit of a dodgy back and can't be arsed attitude. She does not pick up her feet properly and falls to her knees, kicks the toes out of her back hoofs, she only wears front shoes. It is my responsibility and privilege to care for her now as she has cared for me over the years. Much to her distaste, I take her for walks. Bloss does not understand the need for this new activity. She is not impressed. Used to carrying me she now opts to protect me as we walk along. Placing herself between me and cars, not to mention seeing off any human massacring leaves and the ever-threatening wheelie bins. She is more observant seeking landmarks around our more frequented routes. She is not fast, and we plod along at a snail's pace content in each other's company. Local people are confused at the concept of my walking the horse not realising their need for stimulus and exercise. When Blossom gets bored, she gets naughty (if she musters the energy) and I do not enjoy dealing with the aftermath of her escapades. We are sometimes joined by our meanders by dogwalkers venturing in the same direction. We share anecdotes of our respective animals, natter about the weather and breathe in the cold. Bloss accepts the attention; horses are social creatures, they get lonely. It always ignites a warm fuzzy feeling when your horse is happy to see you. Obviously, the joy is closely linked to the food buckets you provide, but I willingly suspend this belief, and through rose-tinted glasses see friendship and affection. The unfortunate reality is that Blossom is not going to last forever. The vet has refused to remove her head (after death may I add) so I can taxidermy and preserve her beautiful face. At some point, as with anything alive, she will drop from this mortal coil. I do not want to consider this, not yet.

     We have been together for 15 years. She is my greatest love and achievement. But my elegant childhood pipe dream is just that.

     Needless to say, in the years I have had horses they have cost me money. So much money. Time, friendships, social life, and feminine hands. They are hard work and sometimes there's little reward. As an owner, you are not only responsible for the animal, but you are also responsible for their excrement. Like the horse, this is a commodity and out of interest I made some calculations. With prices settling at around £50 per cubic metre of well-rotted manure the current value of my muck heap stands at approximately £2800. It seems that in rich in shit.

Left-Hand Path

Pens are designed to be pulled along the paper, allowing the ink to dry as the nib moves forward and away. For the left-handed writer, this is no easy task. We push the pen along. It snags and judders. Pressure cannot be applied. Ink sputters from the end of the nib as it fights to stay together. The slim metal halves opening slightly as it forges its path. It will not know the comfort of the effortless pull and glide.

glibble (noted)

Studies on left-handers have shown they are more susceptible to lifelong psychological problems, depression, schizophrenia, ADHD and autism. Left-handed girls are rarer than left-handed boys. My sister and I are the only left-handed members of the family.

We were united in our oddity. Aged thirty-four I was recommended to have tests for ADD and autism. Initial results indicated I have both conditions. I decided that I have overcome so much without these labels I would remain with the one I preferred to own ... weird.

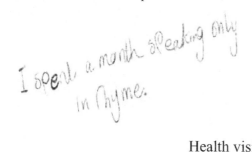

I spent a month speaking only in rhyme.

Health visitors explained my mind was too busy. Overstimulated. That's why my imagination terrified me in my dreams. It ran riot. It still does. I obsess over things, always have. Most obsessions ended quickly. A flurry of intense interest that flatlined at its peak.

Kay Newed

I could read a secondary level prior to starting primary school. I didn't realise this wasn't normal. Words led to worlds where I fitted, or I could disappear into realms that I could never otherwise imagine. When my imagination was fed, my anxieties were lessened. I was absorbed into literature.

My love for animals and nature, history, learning and creativity has never waned. Music classes came and went as most instruments catered for the right-handed. Roller skates caused too much blood, Brownies and Drama Club were abandoned as my clumsiness became a focus of ridicule. I became frustrated, withdrawn, aware of my ineptitude. Why couldn't I do simple things? I had to ask for help with buttons, with unscrewing bottles, whilst those around me flaunted their dexterity. I struggled with words. Lines disappeared in my hands. I couldn't see what was happening. Words became lost, smudged away by the side of my hand and smeared across my pages. A darken oval proof of the movement of the pencil onto my skin.

cuddly-writer

The joy books and words brought me created further anxieties. Would I ever be understood? My marks are ineligible. Illegible.
I relied on speech.
I've never been elegant, delicate, lacking in grace from birth. Words came easily. I spoke at seven months, not the generic Mum and Dad nonsense. Instead, my first word was pretty. Christmas was punctuated by my words. I didn't try them unless I had formed them fully in my jellylike infantile brain. Highly intelligent advanced, but I didn't fit. My brain too busy for its body, for the developmental stages, graphically plotted by the health visitor and educators. My parents didn't sleep, neither did I know the full eight hours until at least seven years old. Overactive imagination causes heightened anxiety and nightmares. Terrors I couldn't articulate. A world that didn't make sense. I was considered unusual. I had an imaginary friend. Joey. He was my playmate, equal, co-conspirator and confidante. He was obviously invisible because he had been cursed by an evil witch in another land. But he was included and had a seat in our treehouse and at the table.

historically, left-handedness is considered a sign of witchcraft, of sinister intentions and untrustworthiness.

Clumsy, awkward, cack-handed. The only left-handed pupil in my class. Simple tasks required the capabilities of a contortionist. Scissors with metal blades were out of bounds. Reading a ruler correctly was impossible, I became an expert at subtraction. I could not write as I could not see what I had written. At school, my paper was taped to the desk to stop me from turning it as I did at home. My teacher desired me to conform. I was not special. At home I created. I made marks that made sense in a convoluted twisted fashion. Curling wrist and paper I could see the marks I was making. And I was understood. I filled pads with words and pictures that eluded me at school. There was magic in my scrawl as it became rounded and smooth, so unlike the angular squashed scratchings rendered between nine and three-thirty. Rushed and panicked to get down a phrase whilst it was fresh in my mind.

 I was not allowed pens because of the mess I made. Years spent wielding a black and yellow striped HB. This is still the only pencil I consent to use.

 Pencils are more forgiving than ink. They are erasable. But I never use them sharp. Always slightly blunt the newly sharpened point, gently round it. Now it can move with much less risk. Grey, pale grey marks snake cautiously across a carefully ruled line. Crisp, black and three centimetres apart they run parallel across the page. In between these lines, my words are meant to fit. With the paper taped immobile to the desktop, I could not see them beneath my fingers clenched around that pencil.

 Pencil smudges. I would lightly touch it to the paper to try and stop this. To stop the smear of my awkward left-hand ruining what I had painstakingly written so light it was barely visible. The grey patch on the side of my hand grew darker. Evidence of the words illegible on the page. My letters would trespass over their predetermined perimeters. My handwriting never improved.

 As others were presented with a Berol Handwriting pen I stayed stoically with my black and yellow pencil. A baton of shame amongst the plastic lidded tools of my classmates. I coveted that pen. That plastic cylinder with its blue pointed tip and a lid that snicked on and off. I agonised over it. I practised with any pen I could get my hands on. Ink smears and is not erasable. The side of my hand became a mottled collage of black and blue smudges which I would rub onto my clothes to hide my failure.

Mrs Cousins was a woman you tried to obey. The evil stepmother in all the fairy tales. She was the ultimate harridan. The villain in my story. The inspiration for Miss Trunchbull, Professor Umbridge with a dash of the Witch of the Waste thrown in. She was contained in a uniform of tweed and jumpers knitted by goblins with roughly spun wool with a bit of barbed wire and camel's hair thrown in for good measure. I weaved her tale as Rumpelstiltskin spun straw. Here was a woman with an iron heart to match her rivet welded underwear. She creaked when she walked, breathed heavily and analysed her subjects through steel-framed glasses which homed in on every insecurity and eccentricity dwelling within these small malleable children. I was doomed.

My handwriting never improved

My accidental misdemeanours hung like a neon sign above my head, a huge pulsating arrow singling me out for special attention. Systematically I was broken down. My quirks and inabilities highlighted and used as an example. A day without being allowed to write with my left hand on Victorian day culminated in a dunce's hat, but at least being in the corner meant I was out of the way. My imagination was quelled, enthusiasm boxed and shelved. I knew I was a 'weird child', and already a perfect target for bullies without the authority figure signalling oddities to

my handwriting never improved

taunt. My inability to grasp the concept of left and right, my prodigious grasp of language and empathy and my fascination with any little living thing was openly mocked. I was clumsy, lefthanded awkwardness meant I was either a goal post or stopwatch monitor rather than an active participant. I lost myself in books, insentient creatures both dead and alive, art and David Attenborough documentaries.

Children are cruel, adults more so. Adults in a position of power can be tyrannical. Mrs Cousins was the cause of many sleepless nights. Her reprimands and disapproval echoed in the ears of those around.

Do you want everyone to think you're stupid? Everyone else can do it. I thought you would have learnt by now.

I was not stupid. I was advanced, I could articulate, reason, expand upon answers. I just struggled to write. I hoped she would one day be taken away and get her comeuppance. A demise fitting for a wicked witch or evil stepmother. I believe she retired. A carriage clock with engraved dates ticks away upon a mantle.

I painted and drew prolifically. Colours, textures and shapes were a language I could master. The only perimeters being the edge of that page.

My grandfather was an artist, musician, craftsman. He spent hours trying to teach my backward fingers to make sounds as well as shapes. Music was a language I loved but could not create. A variety of lessons were booked and abandoned. Instruments gathered dust.

One day, he presented me with a small box. Elongated. Simple. It was the start of summer. I had graduated to metal scissors, sewing needles and biro. This is new, he told me, and this will be difficult, harder than anything else so far. Because this will make you think because you will want to succeed in this. This tiny thing is the best weapon against everyone who doesn't believe you can. Inside on a soft fabric board, held with black elastic was a pen. It was the length of my hand, wrist to fingertip. The girth of my fourth finger. Sleek, silver in colour, tapered at the end. Cold to the touch but filled with energy and promise.

My grandad handed me a belief that I was capable and worthy of beautiful writing. He handed me the tool that made me want to prove those who had kept me at pencil level wrong. I was ten.

A cartridge pen poses difficulties when you're not able to unscrew things easily. Let alone insert and apply the correct pressure to said cartridge. I spent my summer ink spattered, smudged. Mechanics' blackened fingernails had nothing on mine as I toiled away and retaught myself writing. Free expression where before there was a struggle is a wonderful thing. Overcoming inability, problem-solving, alternative thinking. Apparently, the traits of the lefthanded population. Necessity is the mother of invention. Turning the page means that I can see what I'm doing. I write completely horizontally. I also turn the page, so the lines track uphill. A 45-degree angle allows my writing to elongate and slant. A spider dipped in ink saunters across the page.

I returned to school, and a different class. There were no pencils. There were no taped down pages. I am invariably ink-stained, be it from a pen, tattoo machine or brush stroke.

My pen is central to my writing. It is still present in each notebook, letter, diary. It has travelled with me and recorded my world. These clumsy hands have glided thousands of miles on a puddle of ink over paper.

Words still haunt my dreams. I wake with sentences emblazoned across my psyche. They are momentous, exciting and I forget them by morning. Notebooks litter my spaces. I am a stationery hoarder. In the darkness, I reach for a prepositioned notebook and pen. Find a page and hope it will be legible. Pages with layers of letters as ideas have stacked up. A lattice of words I muster and keep. I no longer dwell in childhood make believes. The lines between hero and villain are layers like my three am pages. The devils sits upon my left shoulder. Ink gathers on the side of my left hand. I am powerful with it. The pen is mightier than the sword. I am fully armed.

Why Weight

I am in an abusive relationship. It is one I cannot control, and from which I cannot escape. Nor do I want to. I am aware of the damage. The endless cycle of harm, misuse and guilt. That inevitable promise of it never happening again, this will be the last time, I love you, we will get through this. All the clichés wash over me, followed by care, kindness and acceptance. These periods vary in time and regularity, but ultimately, they do not last. I return to the murky loathing, the criticisms, denials and depression which are now woven into my normality.

Within this hatred lies love, and that is what I keep hold of. I love my abuser. I am reliant upon them for my happiness as well as my hurt. For all the positives, those grasped opportunities, the choices that have put me on wonderful paths. For all the chances to explore me as a person and for being allowed to fail as well as succeed.

My abusive relationship is not unusual. It is abnormally common. People live with these relationships unaware. It is dangerous. Because my abuser is me, and I have learnt to admit it.

I consider my body and the wonderful thing that it is. It does whatever I need it to do, attempts to do things that I know it will not achieve. For this I berate it. I look at the flaws and inabilities in my body as an enemy which must be destroyed. That nemesis will be thwarted and punished so that I can move forward and succeed. I deny it adequate sustenance or fill it with junk and expect it to perform. It is kept in pain, under stress, exhausted. I am aware of my relationship with food, and how toxic it is. I am aware of my bad choices and the consequences, which means punishment. I put myself through hard training programmes, which hurt, and will hurt for days to come because I have become indoctrinated with the belief that this is good pain. This is pain that leads to improvement. It is proven that overweight and obese people face stigma and discrimination regarding employment education and healthcare. We are stereotyped as lazy, unmotivated, slovenly, impoverished. My poor mental health was instantly diagnosed as a result of my obesity. The direct result of living within a fat body. Indeed, every ailment I had was caused by my weight. The belief that my weight was the root cause of all my unhappiness became more and more justified, underpinned by health professionals, educators and the world around me. I was fortunate enough to grow up without social media and the pressure it expels directly from the palms of our hands, but I knew my body didn't fit, literally, in the space it had been assigned.

    My physical self-abuse is directly influenced by my mental health, and my mental health can be tracked photographically through my fluctuating frame. Looking back through pictures there are times of extreme happiness alongside the darkest of times. Extremes mirrored by extremes, and neither end of the scale is healthy.

    My weight has been problematic since childhood. I remained composed of circles as my peer's puppy fat melted away revealing sleek greyhound-like limbs that frolicked in playgrounds and ate up the ground as they chased footballs and peddled bicycles breakneck along the avenue. Ever awkward I tried to keep up, following along, red-faced, puffing, ballooning cheeks always last. In the PE line-up, chosen last or second to last with the other fat child in the class. Each embarrassed with pleading tear brimmed eyes, looking to the team captains desperate to be valued more than the other.

I tried too hard, a trait that continues today. I try hard for acceptance in a world where face value is a universal currency. My self-depreciation was instilled young. Unfortunately, my sister was one of those childhood whippets. Blonde, blue-eyed, easily funny and likeable, I was eclipsed by her in many ways. I was compared to my sister. This was not her fault, but it has affected our relationship. I have a vivid memory of my Grandma Bumble saying with deep concern to my sister 'You shouldn't eat all those, you don't want to be fat like Deelee.' A flippant remark I was never meant to hear, but one that has burned its way into my subconscious like a superheated ball bearing through ice cream. I wasn't even enough for those who were meant to love me. Instead, I was too much. I was ashamed of myself and embarrassed for them.

I dreamt that one day my curse would be lifted, that I would be able to do monkey bars, that the swing chains wouldn't cut into my thighs, that I would be picked, not first, but third or fourth. I truly believed from my interpretation of a rudimentary skin cross-section diagram in the nurse's office that I could make a cut in my stomach. The fat nestled just underneath. I could use a spoon and scoop out all the fat, but it would have to be long-handled and shallow to be most effective. I needed that specific spoon. I was certain that thinness would mean happiness and I unhealthily pursued it.

I have spent most of my life on a diet. When I was thirty, I decided that I really needed to do something. Thirty is an age that I dreaded and one I was determined to enjoy. The death of my uncle at thirty made me realise the fleeting nature of time. I had spent too much of it unhappy. I dieted and trained hard, for months. It became obsessive and driven by a combination of desperation and an addiction to people's approval. With each kilo I lost I was praised. I was suddenly worthy of notice, I was valid. Yet I was very unwell. I dropped forty kilos. I should have felt amazing, but I felt exhausted, confused. I stumbled over words, forgot things, was in constant pain. Things that had previously been considered weight-related were worsening. At sixty-eight kilos I returned to the doctor, who dutifully did my BMI and said I could easily lose another seven, but he would investigate my fatigue, abnormal menstrual cycles and discomfort. Now, these things could not be attributed to my large and unhealthy body. I was sick. I suffer from hyperthyroidism, polycystic ovaries, fibromyalgia, chronic fatigue syndrome and OSFED as well as bipolar and anxiety.

    Diagnosis with any long term or life-changing condition means suddenly you become powerless. There is no control. You must succumb, it is terrifying. I felt instantly guilty for all the mistreatment I had put my body through. All the deprivation of love and nutriment. All the bad relationships I allowed to happen because I felt I didn't deserve better. My body was already suffering, and I was willingly maiming it, I didn't appreciate it when it was well. The realisation that my lifestyle needed to change was something I was unwilling to consider. I was acccpted in this thinner frame, but the regime needed to maintain it was unrealistic. These problems were not solely caused by my weight, some of them had caused it. The knowledge that I had the condition became eclipsed by the treatments for it. The multiple concoctions of medications would immobilise me for weeks. Only able to get up and see to Blossom before returning exhausted to bed. The weight which had taken 12 months to lose was regained within 2, and with that, my mental health deteriorated. Where there was little space for a larger body, where would there be space for a larger and less able one? A complicated body with additional needs. This stage of self-pity was valuable in my recovery, and in hindsight, I am pleased I allowed myself to have it. there is huge pressure to make the best of things, to always look to the positives in situations and move forward. But sometimes you need to stop and admit that it's all fucked up and that you're angry, and frustrated and for you, at that moment it's the worst place to be. I was aware that other people were worse off, we all are, but for that time I couldn't care, and I cried repeatedly for my nonfuture.

    I grieved for my unrealised future. The one where I could run 10km without pain, buy clothes from Topshop, knew I could fit into a space that previously I would spill out of. My work tattooing was thwarted as I lost concentration and feeling in my hands. I couldn't work, write, paint or ride. As my identity diminished my weight and depression increased like a taunting balancing game. And I was angry. Angry at doctors for not taking me seriously for so long. Angry that I hadn't done more with my 'healthy' time. Angry that I had treated myself so badly. And that now I was less likely to fit into any society made mould.

    So, despite my pain and fatigue, I returned to the gym and conscious food choices. But instead of using it as a weapon to punish myself for that packet of Jaffa cakes, the inhaled Mars bar, extra toast at breakfast, or like now the Maltesers I chose over the fruit bag in the meal deal. (I got a smoothie, so it balances out right?) Now it is a tool that I can use against my condition. I can try to be as healthy and strong as possible, then I will not be as affected by my illness. This attitude baffles many. I have the perfect excuse not to go to the gym. The perfect excuse as to why I'm not slim. Why do I stay working when I could claim sick? Why do I study and write when I lose words and cognitive function at the drop of a hat? I do these things because I am not defined by my body and its limits. If I keep doing as much as I can then my future is not a bleak as I first believed.

Despite my new attitude, nothing was stable. However, much I tried to be accepting and receptive of my new body I was frustrated by it.

We are dandled in a state of constant anxiety. A state where we are shown we are not good enough, but also placed on a pedestal of beauty and worth. Bombarded by images of extremes, it is a constant struggle against ourselves. It is capitalised on. I bought diet pills, meal replacements, followed regimes with celebrity endorsements. I wanted the before and after miracles. The promise that everything is better once you conform to society's stereotype. Money flows from our insecurities.

It is a huge business, and we are exploited. Gym memberships, supplements, specific foods, exercise DVDs. All things I buy into. I follow lifestyle bloggers, Instagram influencers from all angles. Body positivity pioneers and healthy lifestyle promoters. They use the same tools. Spew the same rhetoric. The same messages. Fuelling the same anxieties. Keeping alive the same questions.

It is evident that fat-shaming does not aid weight loss, but in the early 1990s body positivity was not as visible as it is now. I looked to the body positivity movement. The concept that we should be accepting of ourselves and our bodies for the wonderful things that they are is for many inspirational. I agree with the sentiment that we should not be criticised or shamed for our bodies not being 'perfect'. Beauty ideals have evolved through history. We need only to look at icons such as Marilyn Munroe, Elizabeth Taylor, Naomi Campbell, Dita Von Teese, to see changing fashions. Now the rise of the 'plus size' is upon us, but I am unsure if this is any less damaging than the heroin chic of the 1990s, or the wasp-like corseted eras gone by.

I am not disrespecting those that take pride and

pleasure in their size, those who are in love with their bodies regardless of weight shape or ability. But how can anyone love themselves and be wholly accepting of themselves all the time? I know that as a species, humans are becoming larger. We are becoming heavier. Hurrah for sedentary lifestyles and easy accessibility to food. Two-thirds of Britons are overweight, and the normalisation of this is prevalent on social media and within the body positivity movement. Yet even if it is becoming more common, does it mean we should be fully accepting of it? I have been at both ends of the scale, within the destructive grip of eating disorders and obesity, and I can say that neither is recommended. I wonder why it is acceptable to celebrate obesity when anorexia is condemned. Each is a disease. Each focus on the external. The façade. The look. But my perception as an overweight individual is that the body positivity movement is inadvertently dangerous. By vilifying those who continue to struggle with body image the movement asks us to accept our flaws. I accept my flaws, but I am frustrated by them. I still dream of that long-handled spoon that will magically scoop out my unwanted rolls and flatten my dimpled thighs. It is unrealistic. Instead of feeling like a failure for not being thin, I feel a failure for not loving being fat. For not loving all the faults with my body. I now have a right to demand room for my size, but not a right to demand room for my insecurities or frustrations. These emotions are invalid in a sphere where they should be most visible.

You can be fat or thin, but the focus is still on how you look, not your capabilities, intelligence or worth. Celebrating obesity is irresponsible. It is unhealthy. My obesity stemmed from my addiction to food. I caused my obesity which was then exacerbated by my poor mental and physical health. Yet ultimately, I was responsible, and I am responsible for my recovery. Accepting obesity as a positive state is irresponsible. By celebrating the result of a disorder, the underlying causes are overlooked. We are not allowing space to say, 'this is why I am not happy, this is what has caused my weight, and I want to change it'. Looking back through my journals I lost count of the entries promising to be better, to lose weight, to look after myself, to try harder. yet I had not considered the source of the problem, only the result. Losing my weight and accepting my flaws was a step on a long journey to discover my self-worth. I allow myself days where I hate everything about myself, from my greying eyebrows to my stretch-marked tummy. I do not apologise for these days. Neither do I apologise for the days where I feel incredible. When my skin glows and I feel strong, toned and most of all, worthy. These days are becoming more frequent as I continue to build a different future which my illness will mould.

    People have always faced marginalisation. There has always been fear of the 'other', whether that is physical, psychological, gender-based, or religious. Humanity has a way of wheedling it out and exploiting it. We need only look to our recent past where those with mental health issues were incarcerated and subject to horrific torture, those with physical disabilities segregated from society. Luckily most of humanity are educated and aware. Most, but not all. Acceptance and celebration surround the diversity of individuals. And with social acceptance, there arises the pressure for personal acceptance, and this is where I remain very much in conflict. I refuse to apologise for my conflict.

Acknowledgements

I would like to thank all those who have encouraged me to create this book.

To my family and friends, who I have driven insane with my wittering's.

To those who have guided its development, have read, and reread Making Marks a number of times, and those whose assistance in research was invaluable.

Thank you for all the experiences that have made this work possible.

Printed in Great Britain
by Amazon